AF414416

A'Mused

Jared Exenberger

BookLeaf Publishing

India | USA | UK

A'Mused © 2023 Jared Exenberger

All rights reserved.

No part of this publication may be reproduced, stored in a retrieval system, or transmitted, in any form or by any means, electronic, mechanical, photocopying, recording, or otherwise, without the prior written permission of the presenters.

Jared Exenberger asserts the moral right to be identified as the author of this work.

Presentation by *BookLeaf Publishing*

Web: www.bookleafpub.com

E-mail: info@bookleafpub.com

ISBN: 9789357691697

First edition 2023

DEDICATION

To Ember

A'Mused

A'mused

Every girl should be A'mused
If a man so does choose
To oh! so use them as a muse

Even when she has refused
After he has paid his dues
Failing to comprehend the obvious clues

A fantasy I hope she's excused
How is this still not news?
Her essence is all he views

Jared Michael Exenberger

He laughs in a puff of smoke

He laughs in a puff of smoke
At the differences between
A firm touch and a cool crush filter

They both still give you cancer
The one just pretends to taste a little better
I prefer choking to a firmer touch

- Jared "the smoke" Michael

Borrowed from the blue

As you borrow from the endless blue
Trust you'll be returned to a beach of white
sands
Relax and rest, accept the pulling waves
Floating through the vast horizon

When there's air
Take a breath and keep

Watch the clouds that follow
Shrouded engulfed in sorrow
Regain your strength...
Maybe tomorrow

Slowly reach down into the deep

When your feet find grip
Pulling through the blue of your mind

Relax and rest
Let yourself roll...
It tumbles you round and around
Relax let yourself slip...

When there is strength go deep

Seek and when found
Go back whole to the grain
While you may borrow from the blue
Remember to look and return to the white sand

Even if it's only tomorrow...

 - Jared Michael

Through Eveleigh's Grace

Maybe this is the time I finally get to go home
But that old house is still so far far away
And this whole world has lured me I'm astray

Eveleigh, I pray your glades open to this song
Olivia, I'll save these shoes you've embraced
I'll see that grey gate outside my childhood
home

Although I know just how I'm going to get there
I can't help my wandering aimlessly around
My feet aren't planted wholly plucking through
lonely ground
I've been away... Far away for too long
And I have never seen this vaguely familiar
place
It looks like a memory of somewhere That's
badly traced

Eveleigh, I pray your glades opened to my song
Olivia, I'll save these shoes you've embraced
I see the grey gate outside my childhood home

It's strange to me the "why" I left this heavenly
place

I was a lonely boy but now a longing man
Longing for a home that is not behind me
It'll be good to see Mother Eddie and Sir
Wal'(lace)
It'll be good to play and sing Travis's song
would've been good to greet my old protective
Shel…(don)
It'll be good to breathe comfortably safe and
sound

Eveleigh, I prayed your glades would open to
my song
Olivia, I paid with tattered shoes you did brace!
Standing by the grey gate outside my mother's
home

How can I go? when I've lost my only home
This is just a house now and I'm a different man
Looking for grace with her warm enduring
embrace
Wife I pray to meet where two can make such a
home

- Jared Michael

Spare a talent

Spare a talent?

Spare a talent for me
Woe for me (woe the ex-leper!)
For I once was the greatest
But he took from me my only chance
To win with but a single glance

Spare a talent for me
Woe for me (woe the ex-leper!)
Now my beauty impedes my financial needs
He cured from me my biggest asset
Pity and coin I was truly set

Spare a talent for me
Woe for me (woe the ex-leper!)
I have to beg for a single talent
He stole a talent that needed no rehearsal
My mongrel face coin did place

Allow me to reprise

Spare a talent for me
Woe the ex-lepper (Woe for me)
Developing my skills to a tee

The effort I do begrudgingly
I now have to work to survive

Spare a talent for an old ex-leper
Please I beg (woe the ex-leper!)
allow me to spare none of my sweat
My beauty is now my biggest curse
All I had was my leprosy

I was free (freed from his leprosy!)

Spare a talent for me
Woe for me (woe the ex-leper!)

- Jared Michael

//
Written as a parody of Monty Python's Life of
Brian character the Ex-Leper played by Sir
Michael Edward Palin
//

Oh dear! A too a loo a poo and a Roo!

A little squeeze and I'd smile

Teaching me the funny keys
Oh, for this I'd learn to bellow
Oh dear!! Can't even hear me wheeze

A subtle push and pull; I'd laugh

Learning to play, yes please!
Oh, for this I'd start to wail
Oh dear! Whispering just to tease

A brief refrain... I'd keep step

Playing I'd be at my knees
Oh, for this I'd wager my tail
Oh dear! I'm rhyming this cheese

Oh!...

A quick number, and I'll sing?

Rambling you might feel a breeze
Oh, for me! Babes I'm turning Jell-O

Oh dear! It's about birds and bees

- Jared Michael

Tone it down

Try to hide it
Won't dispute
Not baring a single blow
Unappreciated so leave it be

Tone it down?
Volume won't go!
Like charcoal on snow
Howsit! not going to show?

Tone it down
Things don't change
I know myself well
I haven't felt it, I never will

Tone it down...
Don't draw it out
Risking an unknown chance
Bargaining this Ember to stay

Tone it down
Don't pull too close
For clouds of smoke
Suffocate its melodic glow

- Jared Michael

He descends

He acquired through the unobtainable
A lust for his own breaking heart
As he looks into a darkened mirror
He descends into this art...

(Plays with his own fascination)

Dancing with his whimsical demons
Pleading for his own redemption
Postponing the improbable pact
He descends to yearn...

(For his own eternal revelation)

It pleases an entirely separate part
Needlessly trying to spill it out
Of his own dubiously aligned heart
He descends to learn...

(To fill with joy, his own damnation)

Twisting words for a desired truth
Will only break your imagined heart
Left a scar that bleeds through creation
He descends to Thrive!

(Living with his own charming devastation)

Alluring: the power one gives his own name
He descends like a gift from God,
Outside he goes from his own branded mountain
He descends to love...

(Himself as he sighs a shrug of resignation)

 - Jared Michael

A Poet's Heart

What if I told you of a poet's heart?
And just where you could find it...

He keeps it a secret
Locked away in his chest
Uses it for his craft
Mastered the skill sleeping
Dreaming as she tore out his heart

"The key is to squeeze!
And pour out the art"

Only poets have the key now
And know the secret trick
Descending into the part
All anyone to do is ask
"What do you keep in the chest?"

But beware the poet's key
It might just show you
This masterful skill
And as you start to dream
Sleeping; they'll tear out your heart

It has its own key!
As they pour out the art

- Jared Michael

The wall my friend painted black:

I never knew whose idea it was
To paint the kitchen wall black
They never knew what it would do

And just like flint

Lit a spark with an ember in sight
It was the purest black when I left
When I arrived drawings already started

It finally awoke

Two or three years it had been
Since enjoying a talent begrudgingly repressed
I drew like a child expressing what's within

An astronaut's floating dream

She knew about my creative block
I imagined it like divine intervention
That wall my friend had painted black

Now all that's left

The only thing she couldn't wait to see me finish
In the days after the ember went out, I was
finished
And I won't ever see her light up if she sees it

I regained my art
Found my poetry
Lost a giving Ember
And took a friend away from Ash

It was my Devine intervention

I am sorry

Thank you, Ember, for the encouragement
And thank you Jack, my friend; for painting the
kitchen wall black
It meant the world to me

- your friend Jared

In her wake (Her greatest gesture)

In her wake she had left me at eight
For my life's average; Seven it's always been
She has left but she helped me rejuvenate
Dedication to creation through my being

Left in her wake I hopefully said "Have a good day"
Quietly I thought I heard her say "You must too"
Last thing she said after last night I tried
With a great devastating gesture, I gave

Left in an empty room was my very first intention
Childhood memories; a chest of 12 storybooks
Two she had shared that I postponed returning
She left me at eight in an empty ice-cold room

Left in her wake the heart I had poured on a page
Friendship is what she insisted; That is what I wrote
My last intention; Not even goodbye to a 'friend'?

Love has no exemption; alone I was left in her
wake

She left a parting gift with me in this beautiful
state
Realising too late my heart's on that page as she
read
Even with a love unrequited my duty is to create
Its grounding: In a state she packed up and fled

Beautiful what I knew was left in that empty
room
I still had the two, my first and last intentions
In an empty room the Ten, I had the complete set
I could keep them together my heart in that chest

The greatest poet I ever met, the girl that left me
at eight
Could place my heart in a chest waiting her
return
Stopping checking that burden she had me at
mate
Although, it is now a complete set; my first
intention

In her wake, 12 story books I've placed in that
room
The last intention burning for an impossible
Ember

At least I'm not sitting with my heart in a chest
Waiting in her wake listening for one more hello

In her wake I was left weary and unravelled
She returned while I was away for what she left
A desk, and a few little awkward things
She picked up the chest and then she left

Leaving them on a dresser for the world to see
Like the final piece of cherry twist, I have the
chest
It's my duty to create and give that gesture again
And again, to maybe that encouraging girl, or
Later to my beautiful future children

Now my life's average has been left at eight
I understand that I cannot predict the future
My journeys to finish what I've started to create
And follow my feet to their next destination

 - Jared Michael

For my three dear sisters

The youngest and funniest of three
She was my baby sister at one point
But somewhere through that existence
Living in a house with my troubled soul
I tore away that playful side
When I see her; I still see my baby sister
I feel like she just sees an estranged big brother
Who she could never quite understand
For being a big brother I somehow lost
I miss and love my comical sister Elnay

The middle and sweetest Sister
She would hug me and all I felt was love
We watched movies as she sat on my lap
When I slept on hers, she played with my hair
While me and all three moved here
As we were moving through the air
Somewhere through that existence
Leaving that house with my troubled soul
I tore away her sweetest side
An estranged big brother I became cold, distant
Emotionless never involving her in my life
I miss and love my sweetheart sister Chanté

The oldest and unequivocally pained sister

I admire her strength, enduring due diligence
She could move mountains with her self-faith
She knows what she wants, and she knows she
will get it
I know she knows and has weighed the cost
Life throws her curve balls each and everyday
I've seen her go through hell; I wish I could help
For I was not a big brother to her
When we were younger, I felt we hated
Me somewhere through that existence
When I left that house with my troubled soul
I found a sense of respect and friendship in her
In her dreams and struggles, I'll never doubt her
She may not understand her strange stepbrother
But I miss and love that enduring sister of mine
For I know one day I'll have to call her Dr.
Jeanay

- Jared Michael

Let Miteku take you home

He was the man who had travelled
The charming young prince from Africa
Ethiopia, he keeps while he walks those city
streets
And he taught me the subtle difference

Between "Let me take you back to my place:
you
could stay the night"

And

"Let me take you home! And in the morning I'll
cook you breakfast "

In the morning you'll know!
As you watch him dance
Making eggs like it's a show!
Sunny side up you'll sing
With your hair he'll play
You'll beg him to stay
And he would
The charming young prince from Africa!

Let Miteku, take you home!

Let Miteku, take you home!

Miteku knew the hearts
Of every single love
Let him take you home
Show you his sunny way

Let me take you! take you home!
Let me take you! take you home!

With a prince you'll want a chance
As he fuels your beating heart
You'll wake up with the sun
warm in his sheets!

Let Miteku, take you home
Let Miteku, take you home
Let Miketu with you Dance
Let Miteku hear you sing
Let Miteku play his song

Ethiopia, he keeps as he walks the city streets

I swear on my heart
That this song I stole
The morning after I had heard
As she was dancing down the street
The girl who had this sung.
All the way back to her home!

"Miteku, took me home!"
"Miteku, took me home!"

I swear it

Miteku! Took her home!
Miteku! Took her home!
Let Miteku, take you home!

The charming young prince from Africa

- Jared Michael

Never forget the Bushels:

Watching the pedals of your soul bloom
Love like the blooming flower
Beautifully becoming in the spring
As winter approaches
Bowing, there's nothing but the bushels

See the pedals of soul blossom
Loving as the withering flower
Beautifully radiant in spring
Winter, it bows and will eventually tire
Leaving only the rugged bushels

never forget

Patience, sunlight, water, fresh air
And a mixture of shit
It'll bloom again surviving the blistering cold
Pedals will wilt
be stepped on or
Get picked off the branch
It'll bloom again brighter with a loving heart
That's how florists stay in business

Almost like turning lead to gold

- Jared Michael

My Little Bluebird Ren - for Bukowski

Before reading this read the poem Bluebird by
Charles Bukowski

Seeing my little Bluebird Ren
As it glides out into an imagined sea
I really did enjoy it then
Realizing the truth spoken by Bukowski
He died before I could even live
With the knowledge he did not keep
Of the tortured and creative soul
Or at least the only man to sing it onto paper
More likely; the only thing I let myself hear
Knowing that I am not tough enough
To keep that bluebird in
Letting him out really messed me up
That little Bluebird Ren
But what was left in its wake
I really did enjoy it then
With the guidance of a real poet
An appreciation of my own making
For the vulnerability of a declined heart
Pours out like a leaking faucet
The final answer: a subtle lie
The final question; a beautiful truth

"And it's nice enough" to cry myself to sleep
"But I never weep
Do you?"
Breaks me whenever I need it to

For Bukowski
From Jared

Pandora, the Box and Key

Ah! The naïve Pandora
Unlocked, and looked to see
The now opened box
Why does she leave the key?

Leaving the door just open
Failing she dropped the bloody key
She must have grown up in a barn!
Succeeding it wanders finally free

With or without realising it
Doesn't know what's been done
To unleash on this world
A love that's left untamed

Back when it was battered and blue
Balling, Howling for a new moon
Beautiful: what's bewilderingly unleashed
Burnt electric; turned black as it blinds

To leave with the door just open
Crazy how she dropped the key!
She must have grown up on a farm
Succeeding for thee; free, fawning, finally
battling that beautiful box

Unaware of when and where to share the bloody
key

If it is unrequited...then it must be refined!
It will not search; it won't chase you like a pet
But it will radiate its essence through
Brandishing every little thing its light touches

A lover's grace It wanders to give
To an unbeknownst unkind worldly world
Why! Would there be no one who would want

The wise Pandora fled without the key
For she was too scared to see
The box; opened, unchained, and left wondering
Wandering in an unbeknownst unkind worldly
world

To leave with the door just open
Failing she dropped the fucking key
She must have grown up in a barn
Succeeding I'm finally free

 - Jared Michael

It's easy, then you think!

You see that's the issue
Thinking where
Thinking when
Thinking how
The issue of thinking your problems up

You want to
So, do it
Stop planning
Imaging each step before you decide to take it
Know what you need
List it

You will
So, get to it
Pack your shit
Donate, sell, or chuck what's holding you there
Keep what's special or purposeful
Remove everything else

You won't
Try and stop it
Start with today
You don't become anything; you are what you do
A poet bleeds poetry

An artist brushes art
A singer belts word
It's not about becoming, it's about doing

You are what you do
And if you keep doing it
You get better at it
You master it
You embody it each time you do it
Eventually people see it
What's been in you this whole time
Don't be selfish and hide it from those who'll
call you it if they see it
You are never going to be perfect

 - Jared Michael

The last good fight:

I know this will make sense to few
All the expectations you've been taught to want
out of life
The constant drone of the routine
Slowly but surely muffling out those thoughts
To think you couldn't just pack it or chuck it
To know you'd make something of it
Exactly what it is
You'll only know if you go

I still hear it
The cry of the poet shuffling paperwork
The pain in the painter faking a smile
The joy of a man who loves to meet people
The laughter of man longing for love and the
world
They tell you; you've got it good!
A job you're good at, a steady income, a future
with the company

I'd rather be a horribly dissatisfied man
Knowing I took a shot at being great
Failing knowing I gave it my all
Then stay at "The good company"

Fuck it, I might even settle for "the good
company" one day
I've talked myself into a job before I can do it
again if I find the need, if while I'm sleeping in
my car and this 'good job',' good life' comes
haunting my dreams
Then I will settle for it
Watch myself fail knowing I tried…

But not Before that day

- Jared Michael

Listening for that tone

Never had anything hold me down
Saying I'm doing quite well in tune
Doubts and fears unstrapped from my back
(Oh no)
Wasn't who I am it was all an act

I know that I should have this ability!
But I can sense all your fragility

All the things I've done in the past
Is it even possible for me to ask?
Do think that this would last?
(Oh no!)
Would I have to take off my mask?

It's not like it's ever been easy to start
Well, who knows who's got the key to my heart

Would really like to love you a lot
Not saying that we will work out
Saying at least let's give this a shot
(Oh no)
Knowing we're both filled with doubt

Living in my own world playing a song
Hoping but not hopefully waiting listening for
your tone

- Jared Michael

Oh God! a muse (A'mused Reprised)

My mother knew it was a bad idea
Moving into the room next to mine
Falling unexpectedly into my life
This girl coming from sunshine

Telling her it would be fine
Friends warned me "Don't pursue!"
Told me she'd never be mine
But I still gave the devil his due

My mother's fine-tuned intuition
A girl I knew was always right
Ran from my own stupid imposition
The Sun, it's now out of sight

Fuck I know how I cope
Always just smoking dope
Only thing left is hope
Lol! I'm going rhyme this with rope

This way that I myself amuse
To use love as a muse
Her beauty that I've now abused
Speaking of how I shall this use

Forever in sin; She'll be A'mused

- Jared Michael

A Sonnet: Unrequited but not quite unrefined

Futures that we cannot see
Love that has no bind
Although still a possibility
Devours its way through my mind

Futures with myself? They're guaranteed
Liberation dilutes our expectations
Alas! This is how I am freed!
Doubt blooms its way through creation

Even with odds like these
My Dear, gambling's still a sin
Oddly I still do love a tease
Oh Dear, I'm falling with a grin

For you! I am dubiously inclined
Unrequited but not quite unrefined

- The peculiar friend who shared a wall and in
that madness fell hopelessly in love with you

www.ingramcontent.com/pod-product-compliance
Lightning Source LLC
Chambersburg PA
CBHW070612160726
48003CB00005B/2240